-Awesome-
PAPER PROJECTS
You Can Create

by Marne Ventura

CAPSTONE PRESS
a capstone imprint

Edge Books are published by Capstone Press,
1710 Roe Crest Drive, North Mankato, Minnesota 56003
www.capstonepub.com

Library of Congress Cataloging-in-Publication Data
Awesome paper projects you can create / by Marne Ventura.
pages cm.—(Edge books. Imagine it, build it)
Summary: "Simple step-by-step instructions teach readers how to make original projects from paper"—Provided by publisher.
Audience: Ages 8–12.
Audience: Grades 4 to 6.
Includes bibliographical references.
ISBN 978-1-4914-4293-7 (library binding)
ISBN 978-1-4914-4329-3 (eBook PDF)
1. Paper work—Juvenile literature. 2. Handicraft—Juvenile literature. I. Title.
TT870.V456 2016
745.54—dc23   2015001409

Editorial Credits
Aaron Sautter, editor; Richard Korab, designer; Ted Williams, art director;
Sarah Schuette, studio stylist; Marcy Morin, studio scheduler; Laura Manthe, production specialist

Photo Credits
All photographs by Capstone Studio: Karon Dubke

Design Elements
Shutterstock: Alhovik, Asya Alexandrova, happydancing, M.E. Mulder, R-studio

Printed in the United States of America in North Mankato, Minnesota.
062015   008823CGF15

Table of Contents

Make Amazing Paper Projects!

Take a look around you and see all the ways paper is used. What would the world be like without paper? There would be no lunch bags, no tissues, no newspapers, and no printed books!

But paper wasn't always an easy material to find. It was first invented in China around 200 BC. And it wasn't commonly used until the invention of the printing press in 1456. But soon the paper industry took off and paper mills were built across Europe and the United States. Today paper is found almost everywhere and is often used to make many kinds of crafts.

You don't always need to buy special paper to build some great projects. Take a look around and see what kind of paper you have at home. Then follow the steps and use your imagination to start making paper puzzles, lanterns, models, and even an awesome space station! Let's get started!

Tools Needed

You'll need some common tools to make many of your projects. Gather the following tools and store them in a box so they're easy to find when you need them. Remember to always ask an adult for help when using sharp knives, scissors, or hot glue guns.

scissors	utility knife	hot glue gun	paintbrush
hole punch	cutting board	ruler	yardstick
pliers	paper clamps	rubber bands	

Tips and Tricks

» Get a good cutting mat. Craft stores sell mats with grid lines that help make measuring easy. A wood or plastic cutting board and a ruler will also work well.

» Before starting a project, be sure to read through all the steps and gather all the necessary materials.

Floating Paper Boat

Paper normally isn't very sturdy in water. But with this project you can make a paper boat that actually floats! Build a fleet of these paper boats and get ready to set sail.

MATERIALS

- 8.5- by 11-inch (22- by 28-cm) waterproof paper
- toothpicks

Step 1: Fold the paper in half. Then fold the paper in half in the opposite direction and unfold.

Step 2: Fold the top corners in to the center.

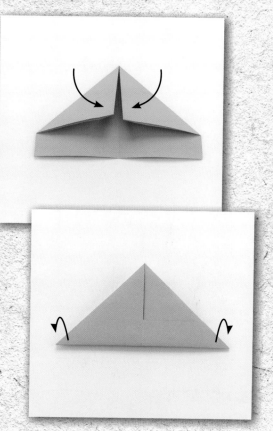

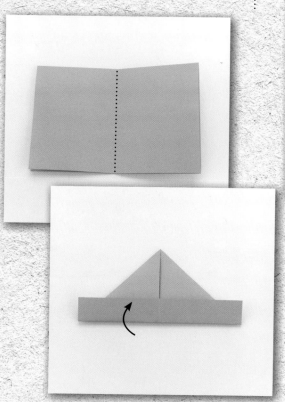

Step 3: Fold the front bottom flap over the base of the triangle. Repeat behind.

Step 4: Fold the corners of the front flap over and tuck them behind the triangle. Turn the model over. Fold the corners of flap over the back.

Step 5: Hold the triangle at the center fold. Pull the sides out to make a diamond shape.

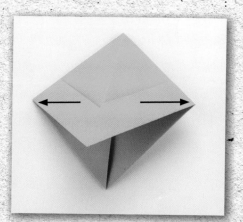

Step 6: Fold the front bottom half of the diamond up. Repeat behind to form a new triangle.

Step 7: Hold the triangle at the center and pull the sides apart to make a second diamond shape.

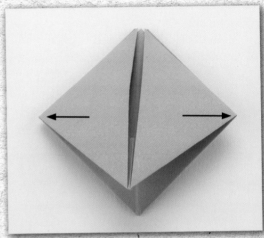

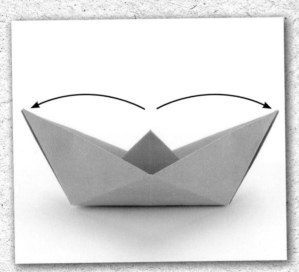

Step 8: To unfold the boat, pull apart the top points of the outer layer of the diamond. Use your finger to form the triangle in the center into a cone shape.

Step 9: Cut out and glue a small triangle of paper to a toothpick. Glue the toothpick to the boat's center cone to make a sail.

Trihexaflexagon

Have fun turning a boring strip of paper into a magical 3-D gadget! With a little creativity, you'll have a cool six-sided figure that can be flipped inside out to form different designs.

MATERIALS

- strip of white printer paper, 1.5 by 11 inches (3.8 by 28 cm)
- markers or colored pencils

Step 1: Fold the left corner of the paper inward to form a small triangle. The folded side should be 1.75 inches (4.4 cm) long. Now fold the pointed corner up to form an equilateral triangle.

Step 2: Flip the paper over and fold a second equilateral triangle. Flip the paper again and fold a third triangle. Keep flipping and folding until you have 10 triangles. Open the strip and trim away the ends.

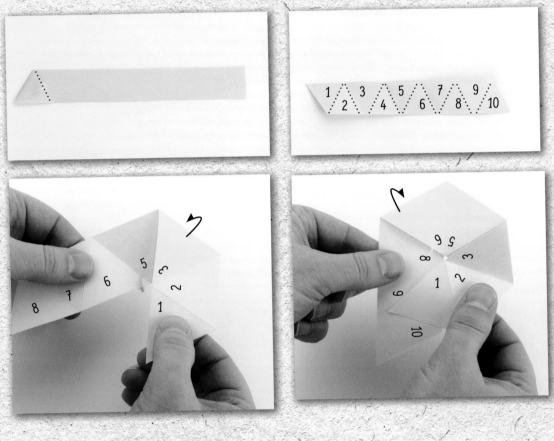

Step 3: Fold the fourth triangle behind the third.

Step 4: Fold the seventh triangle behind the sixth.

Tip: Be sure to flex the hexagon in both directions to see all six designs.

Step 5: Slip the first triangle behind the ninth.

Step 6: Turn the paper over. Then fold the tenth triangle under the first and glue it in place.

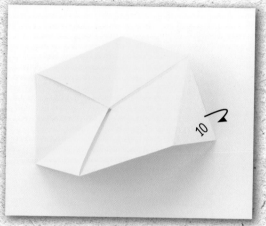

Step 7: Flex the flexagon by pinching the folds inward. Then open it again from the center.

Step 8: Decorate each of the three sides with markers or colored pencils. Now you're ready to impress your friends! Flip your flexagon inside out to show all the different designs.

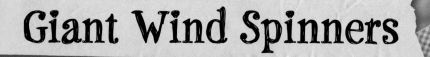

Giant Wind Spinners

Planning a fun-filled get-together or party? With some colorful paper, small dowels, and pins, you can create a festive party mood. Line your yard or porch with these giant spinners and watch the wind make them twirl.

MATERIALS

- colorful craft paper, 12 by 12 inches (30.5 by 30.5 cm)
- wooden dowels
- rectangular erasers
- pins with round heads
- buttons

Step 1: Glue two sheets of paper back to back and allow to dry. Draw a large X on the paper, with the lines crossing at the center. Cut diagonal lines from each corner about halfway to the center of the square.

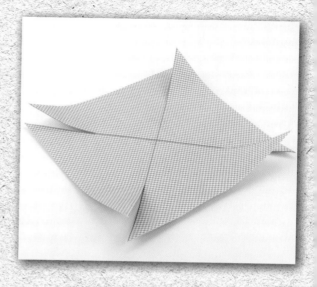

Step 2: Punch a small hole in the upper left corner, just under the cut. Turn the paper and repeat for each corner. Punch a fifth hole in the center of the paper.

Step 3: Cut a 0.5- by 1-inch (1.3- by 2.5-cm) piece off the eraser. Carefully carve a small hole with a craft knife in one side to fit the dowel. Place the eraser on the dowel.

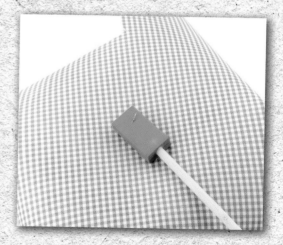

Step 4: Bend the four corners of the paper to the center and line up all the holes. Place the button over the corners. Push the pin through the button and the holes.

Step 5: Stick the pin through the eraser and out the other side. Use pliers to bend the point of the pin back against the eraser.

13

Happy Chinese Lanterns

In China people welcome the New Year by hanging lanterns to light the way to a happy future. You can make these lanterns using any colorful paper you have around the house. Add battery tea lights and light up your room or yard when the Sun sets.

Step 1: For each lantern, cut a 1-inch (2.5-cm) wide strip from the short end of the paper. Save the strips for the lantern handles.

Step 2: Fold the sheet of paper in half lengthwise. From the folded edge, measure and mark several lines 3.25 inches (8.3 cm) long. Make the lines about 1 inch (2.5 cm) apart. Cut along the lines. Be sure to stop cutting at the ends of the lines.

Step 3: Unfold the sheet of paper and roll it into a tube. Overlap the uncut ends and tape them together. Push together the top and bottom of the tube to spread out the lantern sections.

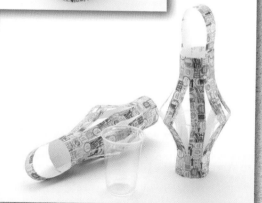

Step 4: Place a plastic cup into the bottom of the tube. Tape it in place. Tape or glue the strip of paper from step 1 to the top of the lantern to form a handle.

Step 5: Turn on a battery-powered tea light and place it inside the plastic cup.

Tip: Make several lanterns and hang them from a long string or wire outside after dark.

15

Awesome Space Station

What is that huge gray globe hanging from your ceiling? Is it a space station? Or is it a giant space-based super weapon? Either way, it's an awesome spacecraft—made by you!

MATERIALS

- 1 sheet of paper, 8.5 by 11 inches (22 by 28 cm)
- 1 8-inch (20-cm) wide paper plate
- 20 sheets of heavy paper or cardstock (silver or gray)
- piece of string, 4 feet (1.2 meters) long
- paper clip

Step 1: Place the paper plate on a piece of paper and draw a circle around it. Cut out the circle.

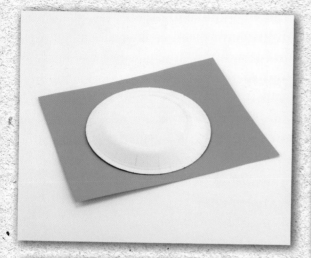

Step 2: Fold the circle in half. Then fold it into thirds and crease the folds. It should look like a slice of pie. Unfold the circle.

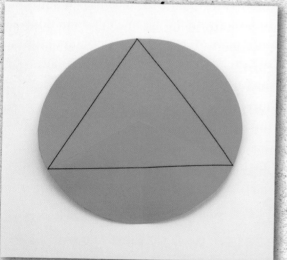

Step 3: Mark every other end point of the fold lines on the circle. Use a ruler to draw straight lines between the points to make an equilateral triangle. Cut out the triangle. This will be your pattern.

Step 4: Use the paper plate to draw circles on the 20 sheets of silver paper. Cut out the circles. Use the triangle pattern to lightly draw triangles inside the circles. Fold each circle along the triangle lines.

17

Step 5: For the top of the station, glue five circles together along the folded edges. This will make a circular shape. Repeat with five more circles to make the station bottom.

Step 6: Glue the remaining ten circles side by side to form a straight line.

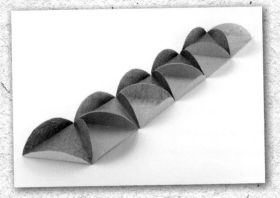

Step 7: Glue the two ends together to form a ring. Then glue the top and bottom pieces to the ring to form a sphere. Do not glue the last two sides together yet.

Step 8: Tie the string to a paper clip. Glue the paper clip in place inside the station. Leave the rest of the string outside the sphere. Glue the final two sides together and allow all the glue to dry completely. Now just hang your space station in your room for an awesome decoration.

Tip: You can make your space station more realistic by using markers to add details like seams, bolts, doors, and hangar bays.

Puzzling Paper Cubes

How do you transform six squares of flat paper into a 3-D cube? Find out with this amazing puzzle cube. Once you learn how to fold the first piece, it's easy to fold five more. The challenge is in fitting the folded pieces together.

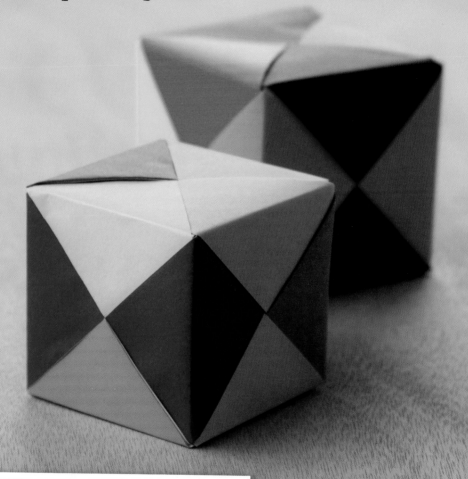

MATERIALS

• 6 squares of colored origami paper, 6 by 6 inches (15 by 15 cm)

Step 1: Fold a square of paper in half. Crease and open.

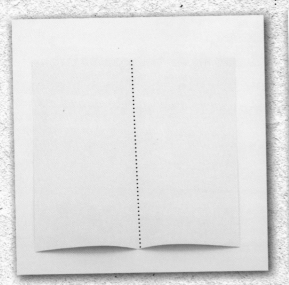

Step 2: Fold the right side in to meet the center crease. Repeat on the left side.

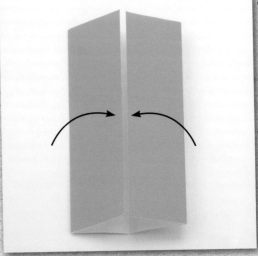

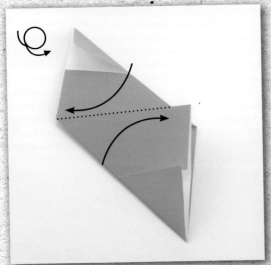

Step 3: Turn the paper over. Fold the lower left corner up to meet the right edge. Fold the upper right corner down to meet the left edge.

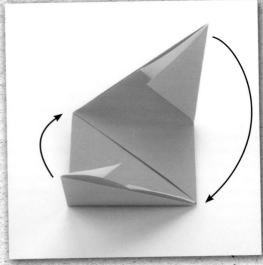

Step 4: Turn the model 90 degrees clockwise. Fold the top triangle down and the bottom triangle up to form a square. Crease all the folds well and let go. The piece will have a square in the middle with triangles standing up on the top and bottom.

Step 5: Repeat steps 1–4 to make 6 pieces in different colors.

Step 6: Slide a triangle from one piece into an opening of the square on a second piece.

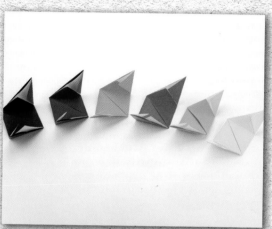

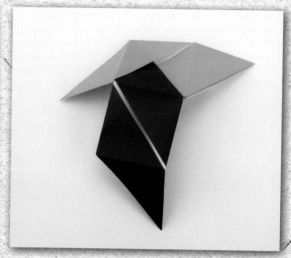

Step 7: Slide a triangle from a third piece into the opposite opening in the square of the first piece.

Step 8: Keep adding pieces onto each other until you have a colorful cube.

Tip: Make the pieces for another cube for a friend. Give him the pieces and a finished cube. Then see if he can figure out how to make the pieces fit together.

Jolly Roger Pirate Balloon

Who says that pirates sail only in ships? This Jolly Roger balloon warns others that tough sky pirates are on their way. Prepare to defend yourself, mateys!

MATERIALS

- 1 large balloon
- newspaper
- plain paper
- white glue
- painting tray
- flexible wire, 12 inches (30.5 cm) long
- string
- black and white acrylic paint
- small paper cup

Step 1: Blow up the balloon and tie the end. Tear newspaper and plain paper into 2- by 2-inch (5- by 5-cm) squares. Make enough squares to cover the balloon three times.

Step 2: Mix ½ cup (120 milliliters) of white glue with ¼ cup (60 ml) water in a plastic bowl. Pour enough into the painting tray to cover the bottom.

Step 3: Dip a newspaper square into the glue mixture and get it completely wet. Squeeze the paper between two fingers to wipe off the excess glue. Stick the paper to the balloon. Repeat this step to cover the balloon with paper squares. Overlap each square a bit so you can't see the surface of the balloon.

Step 4: Repeat step 3 with plain paper squares to cover the balloon with a second layer. Using plain paper will help you see the difference between the first and second layers.

Step 5: Repeat step 3 to make a third layer using newspaper squares.

Step 6: Tie the knotted end of the balloon to a piece of string. Hang the balloon up and allow it to dry completely. This will take 2 to 3 days.

Step 7: After the paper is dry, pull the knotted end of the balloon away from the dried paper. Pop the balloon with a pin. Pull out the balloon pieces and throw them away.

Step 8: Trim the opening at the base of the balloon to make a 2- to 3-inch (5- to 7.6-cm) wide hole. Use a hole punch to make four evenly spaced holes around the edge of the opening.

Step 9: Use a sharp pencil to make a small hole in the top of the balloon. Make a small loop in the end of the wire. Thread the wire through the hole from the inside of the balloon. The small loop will help hold the wire in place. Make a large loop in the wire on the outside to use for hanging the balloon.

Step 10: Paint the balloon with black paint. When it's dry, add a skull and crossbones on the front with white paint.

Step 11: Punch four holes around the top of the paper cup. Paint the paper cup to look like a basket.

Step 12: To attach the basket, tie four pieces of string between the holes in the cup and the balloon. Now your pirates are ready to launch!

Tip: If you don't like pirates, you can paint the balloon in other ways. Try painting one with a flag or the logo of your favorite sports team.

Hopping Paper Frogs

Did you know a flat piece of paper could become a hopping frog? It's easy to do, and any paper you have will work. Once this frog is folded, just push down on its backside to make it take a leap.

MATERIALS
- 6- by 6-inch (15- by 15-cm) squares of green paper
- marker

Tip: Use different sizes and colors of paper to make an army of hopping frogs. Have frog races with your friends.

Step 1: Fold the paper in half corner to corner to make a triangle pointing up.

Step 2: Fold the lower left corner up to the top point. Repeat with the lower right corner to form a diamond shape.

Step 3: Fold the left point of the diamond to the center. Repeat for the right and bottom points. The paper will now look like an open envelope.

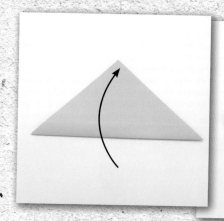

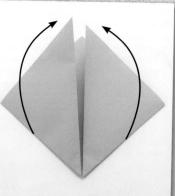

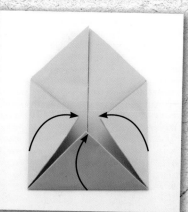

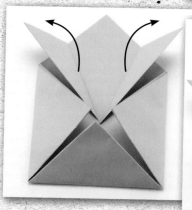

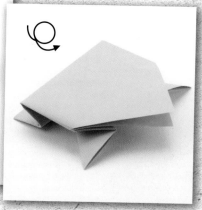

Step 4: Fold the left top flap to the left. It will overlap the left upper edge of the envelope. Repeat with the right top flap on the right side.

Step 5: Fold the bottom of the envelope up at the point where the seams meet. Then fold the top half of this new flap down to meet the bottom edge.

Step 6: Turn the model over. Draw eyes on the frog with a marker. To make the frog hop, press down on the back end until it flips away from your finger.

Wild Rainforest Diorama

Get ready to go on an adventure! With this awesome 3-D diorama, you'll feel like you're on a real jungle safari. Listen carefully and you can almost hear the wildlife prowling around inside.

MATERIALS

- shoe box with a hinged lid
- small box, such as a tea box
- light and dark green acrylic paint
- cardstock paper
- nature magazines
- brown and green construction paper
- light and dark green tissue paper
- colored pencils or markers
- small twigs and rocks

Step 1: Open the shoe box and stand it on its end. Glue the small box between the back of the lid and the back side of the shoe box. The small box will help make the shoe box stable and keep the lid open.

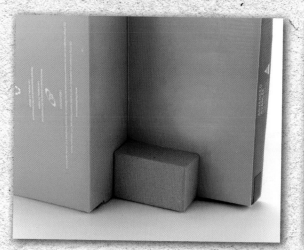

Step 2: Paint the inside of the box. Use dark green at the bottom and light green at the top.

Step 3: Cut out one 7-inch (18-cm) wide rectangle of brown construction paper. Cut out two more 5-inch (13-cm) wide rectangles. Make all the rectangles 1 inch (2.5 cm) taller than the box. Draw a full tree on the large rectangle. Draw half trees on the smaller rectangles as shown. Give the trees a 0.5-inch (1.3-cm) wide tab along the sides and bottoms of the trunks. Cut out the trees and fold over the tabs.

Step 4: Place the trees by gluing the tabs to the inside edges of the box. Glue one half tree to the front of the lid. Glue the whole tree to the center of the box. Glue the other half tree inside the box near the back. Glue the tops of the branches to the ceiling of the box to hold them in place.

Step 5: Cut strips of tissue paper and crumple them to make leaves. Glue the tissue paper to the branches of the trees and the edges of the box. Add enough tissue paper to make it look like a rainforest.

Step 6: Cut ferns and other plants from green construction paper and glue them to the forest floor.

Step 7: Draw and color rainforest animals on cardstock and cut them out. Or glue photos of animals from nature magazines to cardstock and cut them out. Include animals such as crocodiles, gorillas, toucans, tigers, and snakes.

Step 8: Glue the animals to the trees, the leaves, the floor, and the top of the diorama.

Step 9: Add twigs and small rocks to complete your rainforest scene.

Read More

Harbo, Christopher L. *Paper Airplanes: Pilot, Level 3.* Paper Airplanes. Mankato, Minn.: Capstone Press, 2011.

Harbo, Christopher L. *Origamipalooza: Dragons, Turtles, Birds, and More!* Origami Paperpalooza. North Mankato, Minn.: Captone Press, 2015.

Jones, Jen. *Cool Crafts with Newspapers, Magazines, and Junk Mail: Green Projects for Resourceful Kids.* Green Crafts. Mankato, Minn.: Capstone Press, 2011.

Murphy, Pat. *Paper Flying Dragons: Design and Build Your Own Fantastic Flyers.* Palo Alto, Calif.: Klutz, 2012.

Internet Sites

FactHound offers a safe, fun way to find Internet sites related to this book. All of the sites on FactHound have been researched by our staff.

Here's all you do:

Visit *www.facthound.com*

Type in this code: 9781491442937

Super-cool stuff!

Check out projects, games and lots more at
www.capstonekids.com